LETTERS FROM PRISON

Bible Discussion Outlines
compiled by
Branse Burbridge and the I.S.C.F. staff

SCRIPTURE UNION
47 Marylebone Lane, London, W1M 6AX

also in this series

FOLLOWING CHRIST

© Scripture Union 1974
First published 1974

ISBN 0 85421 445 3

Printed by A. McLay & Co. Ltd., Cardiff

CONTENTS

Rome •
Three Taverns •
Forum of Appius •
Puteoli •

DALMATIA

MOESIA

DACIA

ITALY

MACEDONIA

THRACE

Amphipolis Philippi
Thessalonica
Berea • Apollonia
Nicopolis

Troas

Mytilene

SICILY

Rhegium •

Syracuse •

Corinth • Athens •
Cenchreae

Smyrna

Ephesus

ACHAIA

Patmos

Malta •

MEDITERRANEAN   SEA

CRETE
Phoenix • Neapolis
Fair Havens • Lasea

AFRICA

Cyrene •

CYRENAICA

0   100   200 Miles

LIBYA

BLACK SEA

Byzantium

BITHYNIA & PONTUS

GALATIA

KINGDOM
OF
ARMENIA

A S I A

gamum
Thyatira
Sardis
Philadelphia · Antioch (Pisidia)
Laodicea
Colossae
PISIDIA
Iconium
Lystra · Derbe
tus

CAPPADOCIA

Lesser
Armenia

Commagene

Attalia PAMPHYLIA Cilicia
LYCIA Perga Trachea
Patara Myra Seleucia

CILICIA
Tarsus

OSROENE

Antioch

PARTHIAN

EMPIRE

CYPRUS
Salamis
Paphos

SYRIA

Seleu

Babyl

Sidon
Tyre Damascus
Ptolemais Caesarea Philippi
Caesarea
Joppa Samaria
Lydda Judea
Gaza Jerusalem
Alexandria
EGYPT
Nabataean Kingdom

INTRODUCTION

Half the books of the New Testament — thirteen of them, to be exact — have come from Paul's pen. When one remembers that he was tireless in carrying out his commission as 'the apostle to the Gentiles', as well as being passionately devoted to winning his fellow-Jews for Christ, it is amazing that he managed to write any of them. When one thinks of the thousands of miles he must have covered, on foot, in the saddle, on board ship, and the hair-raising experiences he went through, it seems even more incredible.

The fact is, of course, that we owe many of these letters to the greatest privation he endured — imprisonment. Paul's enforced inactivity enabled him to pray earnestly for, and write to, his 'spiritual children' in Philippi, Ephesus, and Colossae, and to at least two individuals, Timothy and Onesimus. In God's mercy he was evidently allowed parchments and ink, and at times he had the help of a scribe, so that his ministry continued effectively in spite of all opposition to his message, to him personally, and particularly to the living Christ within him.

And it continues still. For as we study these same themes from Paul's letters from prison, and apply eternal truth to our own situation, we, too, shall be strengthened and encouraged and our lives will become more Christlike.

This series offers significant and relevant themes within the 'prison letters' rather than a complete study of each book. The intervening sections could be covered by private study.

In order to guard against sameness which can deaden a Bible study group, the series also deliberately varies the approach from one study to the next. It aims to give leaders help where necessary, and they should note the following general points:

1. Study the passages carefully, beforehand, reading them in different translations. Pray as your prepare.
2. For each question suggested, work out possible answers, both your own and those the group are likely to give. Try also to think of some supplementary questions to add to those suggested.
3. Where there is an introduction, it can be read to the group, or put into your own words.
4. Any leader's notes are to help you in your preparation and are not meant to be read out to the group. However, it may be helpful to tell them the particular meaning of a word, before asking questions about the verse where it occurs.

Especially if you have never led a group Bible discussion before, please take note of the hints on how to do it which are printed on some right-hand pages in this book. You will find more detailed information and advice in another Scripture Union publication, *Your Turn To Lead*, by Margaret Parker, which also contains a wealth of outlines and other material.

Outline 1

Paul: the Man Himself

2 Corinthians 5.14-21.

Section A.

It often helps us to understand a person's character, if we know something of his family background and education. In order to deal with this section briefly, make a chart beforehand, and write out the following references on slips of paper for different members of the group to look up: Acts 23.6; Acts 22.2; Acts 22.3 Acts 17.28 (quotation from a Greek poet); Acts 22.27-28; Romans 11.1; Acts 26.4 and 5; Acts 18.3; Philippians 3.5 and 6; Galatians 1.13-14.

Names:
Father's status:
Place of birth:
Languages spoken:
Citizenship:
Nationality:
Tribe:
Education:
Trade:
Religious interest:
Attitude to Christians:

Complete the chart from answers given by group members.

Section B.

Saul's encounter with Christ on the Damascus road resulted in a complete change of direction in his life. His background fitted him for a brilliant career, yet he chose instead a life of hardship.

Why? Read 2 Corinthians 5.14-21. Paul is here speaking from his own experience.

1. In what ways does a man change if he is 'controlled by the love of Christ'?
2. What is the meaning of the word 'reconcile'? How can God and man be reconciled? How much did Paul's background count in his thinking about 'reconciliation'?
3. What did it mean for Paul to be 'an ambassador for Christ'? See 2 Corinthians **1**.8 and 9: **4**.8 and 9: **11**.23-28. What kept him going, in spite of a great deal of opposition and apparent failure? See 2 Corinthians **3**.5 and 6; **4**.7; **10**.18; **12**.7-10.
4. What is Paul's immediate aim? 2 Corinthians **5**.9. And what does he see as God's purpose for his life? v.21. What does this mean in practical terms? Would the fact that he was in prison help or hinder this purpose?
5. If our aim is the same, what kind of life can we expect?

Outline 2:

The Birth of a Church

Acts **18**.24-19. 20.

Ephesus was on the west coast of Asia (modern Turkey). It had a thriving port, wide, well-lit streets, and handsome buildings, including a huge amphitheatre. Its population was probably a third of a million. It was a well-known centre of magical arts and a place of pilgrimage to Artemis, the mother goddess whose temple at Ephesus was one of the seven wonders of the ancient world. There was a Jewish synagogue, and the Christian church sprang from it.

Activity

The leader gives a short introduction, then divides the group into six (if there are fewer than six present some can have two sections). The groups are given passages to read as follows: (1) Acts **18**.24-28 (2) Acts **19**.1-7 (3) Acts **19**.8-10 (4) Acts **19**.11-12 (5) Acts **19**.13-16 (6) Ch **19**.17-20. After three to five minutes, each group sums up in their own words the content of their section.

Discussion questions

1. Is it possible to re-construct the pattern of the birth of the church at Ephesus? What do we learn about the work of the Holy Spirit?
2. Is there a reason for the extraordinary miracles (**19**.11-12) and the dramatic events described in **19**.13-20?
3. Why did the name of Jesus not have the desired effect when used by the exorcists (**19**.13-16)? (exorcist — one who drives out evil spirits).
4. In our own life today, what aspects of magic or the occult oppose the spread of Christian truth? Should we expect more 'spiritual fireworks' than we are accustomed to?

Why Group Study?

Once we have started in the Christian life, we need to grow, and our food is the truth about God revealed to us in the Bible (1 Peter 2.2). But the question may arise — 'Why should we study? Can we not derive our food from listening to sermons and Bible readings?' The answer is that, if we would develop, we must learn to feed ourselves and not be 'spoon-fed', just as a growing child has to do.

'But,' someone may ask, 'is not personal Bible study sufficient? Why should we study in groups?' There are few things more stimulating than tackling a job together with other people; and we help one another to better understanding. Everest was scaled by a team, and each had his part to play. Each member of the group, therefore, should bear in mind that this is a combined effort, and should approach it in a co-operative and helpful frame of mind, not critical of the leader, nor reluctant to contribute to the discussion.

A further important reason for group Bible study is the stress in the New Testament on the importance of fellowship in Christian growth (see for example, Acts 2). The main source of fellowship is, of course, your local Church, and a Bible Study group, wherever it may occur apart from this, is no substitute. At the same time there is nothing quite like studying the Bible together to promote a real sense of unity.

Outline: 3

The Demo

Acts **19**.21-41

Look back first to the notes on *The Birth of a Church* —
at the beginning of outline no 2. The image of Artemis
was alleged to have fallen from heaven, and may have
been a meteorite in roughly female human shape. Terra
cotta replicas have been discovered — the silver ones
must have been similar. The self-interest of the crafts-
men is very obvious, even though it is cloaked in a semi-
religious, semi-patriotic fervour. This is an early example
of industrial action. Clearly the Christian church was
already having a great influence. Sufficient people were
turning away from Artemis to cause a loss of revenue to
the silversmiths.

Activity

The leader gives a short introduction then the passage
may be read in dramatic form. Readers are: narrator,
Demetrius, town clerk and crowd (everyone).

Members of the group then divide into three groups
each to discuss a separate question and to report back
briefly after ten minutes.

Group 1.   Are there any ways in which the Christian
church today is, or should be, influencing commercial
practice? For example, Sunday trading, dangerous over-
loading of lorries, exploitation of teenagers by the 'pop'
industry. . . . In Ephesus there were enough Christians
to organize a boycott. Could Christians do this today?
Should they? If not, what else should Christians do?

Group 2.   This demonstration is an example of mass
hysteria, and was unsuccessful, but crowds can sometimes accomplish what individuals cannot. How useful
and successful are Christian 'demos', and what danger
is there of mass mindlessness?

12

Group 3. Trace Paul's part in all this (21-22, 26, 29-31). Did he approve of the riot? What did he hope to make of this opportunity? Were his friends right to restrain him? What would he have said if he had been the town clerk? What would have been the result?

The leader uses the reports as summing up, or adds a brief summary himself. If there is any time left, discuss the question:

What should be the Christian's approach to industrial unrest? (Be careful to distinguish Christian from party political ideas.)

How to Set About It

There are certain basic principles for Bible study. These are:

(a) to find out what the Bible really *says (some use the term exegesis to describe this).*
(b) to discover the original meaning that God intended (this is sometimes called exposition).
(c) applying this meaning to us today (application).

All three are essential to proper Bible study, whether personal or in a group, for we are trying to find out what *the Bible says* and not to give our opinions or ideas. *It is important to think of the book you study as a whole and to take into account its background and the context in which it was written. Your object will be, not to hunt for hidden meanings, but to understand the plain sense of the passage you are studying, to see the way in which the thought develops, and then from it to work out principles for everyday living. We need to remember that we are dependent on the Holy Spirit, but that does not absolve us from hard work.*

Outline 4:

Be on Your Guard

Acts 20.17-37.

Paul was on his way to Jerusalem, well aware of the dangers that lay ahead. But, as he moved swiftly away from Greece, he had the opportunity of saying his farewell to the elders of the Ephesian church. He had spent over two years there in evangelism and Christian teaching. He was a man in a hurry, and had already decided not to travel back to Jerusalem or Ephesus. It was at Miletus that he sent for the Ephesian elders and spoke these final words — the only example in the book of Acts of a speech delivered by Paul to a Christian community.

Looking back and looking forward   (vv.17-24)

1. List the statements Paul makes in vv.18-21 (also vv. 26, 27, 31, 33), which emphasise the quality of his life and work. (You might like individuals to write them down *or* work them out together on a wall chart). Opposite each statement, try to find a modern 'saint' who demonstrates that particular quality. Discuss the choices you make.

2. What is Paul's chief object in life? (vv.22-24) Do you think his attitude is too life-negating? How can you be sure that your convictions about the future are governed by the Holy Spirit? (vv.22 and 23)

Paul's warning   (vv.25-31)

3. What does he tell them to do? How does this apply to the Christian group we belong to? For example, what difference would it make to our group programme?

4. What does he warn them against? How can we today counter false ideas or inconsistent behaviour in others who call themselves Christians?

Paul's blessing (vv.32-35)

5. What gave Paul confidence that 'the word of his grace' could build up the Christians at Ephesus?
6. Can you suggest practical ways of 'helping the weak' today?

Final Reaction (vv.36-37)

7. What is the place of emotion in the Christian community today?

Preparation (i)

First, pray. Prayer is your top priority:

(a) For yourself as leader
(b) For the other members of the group (by name, if possible)
(c) That, as you prepare, and during the meeting, the Bible may become a living book, teaching and instructing each member of the group.

Next, read the passage from the Bible. If you are using the Revised Standard or Authorised Version, read the passage a second time in a modern translation, so that when you turn back to your other Version you know the meaning of each phrase. It is a good idea to put it into your own words, so that you really understand it. This is the basis of being able to apply its truth, and will enable you to see what the questions in the Outline are 'getting at'.

Outline 5:

Dead or Alive?

Ephesians **2**:1-10

Introduction

Three chapters of this letter are devoted to teaching doctrine. In these verses in Chapter **2**, Paul contrasts the present privileges of the Ephesian Christians with their situation before they were converted.

vv.1-3

1. Ask members of the group to write down in their own words this description of the non-Christian (his relation to God, to Satan, and to himself). Ask for two or three volunteers to read theirs to the group.
2. What do the expressions 'sons of disobedience' and 'children of wrath' suggest about God's nature?

vv.4-10

3. Where does God's mercy stem from, and what has it led Him to do for man? (vv.4 and 5)
   v.6 — 'sit with Him in the heavenly places'. Read chapter 1:20-22. This suggests that Christians are already in a position of victory with Christ.
4. Who or what has been defeated?
   Ask the group to work in pairs and think about the attitude and purpose of 'sitting', discussing whether this picture tells us anything about our new life. After just two or three minutes, share any helpful ideas.
5. Is it significant that the Ephesians are reminded that they are sitting with Him, *before* they are told about their Christian walk (v.10)?

Looking at vv.8-10:

6. Have we any part to play in our salvation?
7. What reasons are there why we cannot alter our relationship to God by good works?
8. But how must our new life show itself?
9. How can we keep this up? (Think back to v.6 and v.8)
10. What does v.10 suggest about the Christian's choice of his sphere of service for God?

Notes for leader

v.1. 'dead' — state of separation from God, i.e. it describes a person without spiritual life, though they may still be physically alive.

v.3. 'flesh' — describes the nature of man not under the Spirit's influence. 'The passions of the flesh' therefore refers to all longings and impulses of the self-centred life and not simply physical desires.

v.3. 'wrath' — the attitude of a just and holy God towards sin.

v.8. 'grace' — God's undeserved favour towards us.

v.8. 'saved' — not only from the punishment of sin but from its power over us.

Outline 6:

Keeping Together

Ephesians **4**:1-16

Paul's teaching in this letter moves now from Christian doctrine to Christian conduct. The word 'therefore' in verse 1 suggests that right conduct should always be the result of right doctrine. Having just assured them in Chapter 3:20 that they have the power to do it, he now begs them to lead a life which is worthy of their calling as Christians. He starts by looking at the corporate life of the Church.

Read vv.1-6

Four qualities are mentioned in v.2. Compare the words used in other translations.

1. For each one, give an example of a situation where that quality could help the smooth working of a Christian fellowship.

(The group could work on this in pairs for two or three minutes only, and then report back.)

In verses 6-6, Paul emphasizes that the church is *already* united. The need is for the unity to be preserved.

2. Do these verses suggest a positive way to deal with differences within a fellowship?

Read vv.7-14

3. What is a) the source b) the purpose of the gifts?
4. Therefore what attitude should we as individuals have to our own gifts, and to those of other Christians?
5. How can one find out what one's gifts are?
6. Is it possible to be too humble about one's gifts?

Read vv.15-16

7. Taking the analogy of the body with Christ as its head, discuss what this teaches us about our dependence on each other and on Him?
8. Does this suggest any changes are necessary in your local church/group/christian union?
9. How could all members of a Christian group be encouraged to feel that they have a vital part to play?

Conclusion

It is significant that Paul uses the phrase 'in love' three times in the passage about unity. Read 1 Corinthians **13**:4-7. Spend a few minutes praying that these qualities of love will be seen in our own lives, and in the churches and other Christian groups represented.

Notes for leaders

v.2 Meekness   —the same word is used to describe an animal under control.

v.11 Prophet   —usually one who 'tells forth' God's word; only occasionally 'fore-telling' events.

v.12 The meaning of the verse is clearer if the commas are omitted; it tells us the main purpose of the gifts.

Outline 7:

New Life

Ephesians 4:17-32

Introduction

In this passage Paul contrasts the life of the Ephesians before they were converted with the life they should be living now. He implies that if there is no change in them, they have not really grasped what Christ has done for them.

Read vv.17-24

1. Is the development of our new life due to God's work in us, or is it our own responsibility? (vv.22-24)
   What part does each play?
   Vv. 17 and 22 imply that the change begins in our minds.
2. What things influence the way we think?
3. What practical steps can we take to keep our minds under God's control?
4. Why is our thinking so important?
5. Split into groups of two or three for about seven or eight minutes. Each group needs pencil and paper.

   In the groups, list (from vv.25-32) all the things which Paul says must be 'put away'. Write opposite each what he says should take its place in the Christian's life. Think of situations at work, at school where each of these instructions should be applied. Do any of them contradict each other? (e.g. v.25 and v.32)

   Briefly compare ideas from the groups.

6. Is there something we can learn from the fact that a positive instruction is given alongside each negative one?
7. What motives has the Christian for keeping these standards? (see vv. 20, 30 and 32)

Notes for leader

v. 22 and v. 24	The tense of 'put off' and 'put on' implies deliberate decision and action.
v.23.	'Be renewed' is passive, and suggests a continuous process by the work of the Holy Spirit.
v.26.	'Be angry and sin not' — this refers to righteous anger against evil, with emotions under control.
v.31.	'Anger' here _is uncontrolled bad temper.

Outline 8:

Who's in Charge?

Ephesians 5:21-6:9

Introduction to whole group

Paul deals with three types of relationships in this section. He introduces it in v.21 by saying that, for any successful relationship there must be giving on both sides (subject to *one another*). Each must be clear what their particular role is in the relationship.

(Leader — This outline will be too long for the whole group to work through. Divide the group into three and give each small group one topic and set of questions to deal with. Ask them to write down answers to the questions and allow at least ten minutes at the end for reporting back. If time, the whole group may like to comment on the conclusions.)

Marriage   Read 5:22-33

Introduction

These verses stress that marriage is a relationship between two equal partners, and shows what the role of each should be. It has been said that, in reading this passage, one should only take note of the verses which apply to oneself!

1. How is the principle of v.21 defined for each partner in vv. 22 and 25?
2. Which role do you think is the more demanding?
3. If this is the nature of the relationship, what qualities would you look for in a partner?
4. Does the end of v.31 ('the two shall become one') imply anything about relationships before and after marriage?
5. (If time) Why does Paul take the amazing step of

comparing the marriage relationship with that of Christ and the Church?

Notes for leader

5:22   'Subject to' does not imply inferiority, but simply defines the role of each.

5:25   'love' — agape, i.e. love which is self-giving, and 'seeks the highest good of others'.

Parents and children   Read 6:1-4

6. v.1. 'For it is right' is the only reason given for obedience. Should this be sufficient for a child, or should reasons be given for rules made?

7. What is the parent's responsibility?

8. This passage is addressed to children. Does this mean there is an age-limit, or can honour be expressed differently towards our parents at different stages in our life? Give examples.

9. What would you do if, being under age, your parents wanted you to visit relatives fairly regularly on Sundays, leaving no time for church?

Notes for leader

6:1   'Obey' — means obedience to commands, and is a different word from 5:22.

6:3   It has been suggested that this promise should not be applied individually, but means that right family relationships lead to stability for a nation or community.

Masters and slaves   Read 6:5-9

Introduction

In the absence of an exact parallel in modern life, we can apply this teaching to the situation of working under authority at school, or in a job. Again the idea of mutual responsibility, and of both parties being under the same higher authority, is brought out in v.9.

10. What motive has the Christian for doing his work to the best of his ability?
11. List the characteristics of a good employee.
12. Are there any situations where it would be wrong to submit to authority?
13. What should a Christian do if the whole of his or her form decided to cut a General Studies period because they thought it was a waste of time?

Notes for leader

6:5 'Obey' — means obedience to commands, and is a different word from **5**:22.

Outline 9:

The Good News for Philippi

Acts **16**.11-40

Philippi, a Roman colony, was situated in a strategic position near the eastern end of a great Roman road which linked the Aegean with the Adriatic. Luke here records what happened when he went to Philippi with Paul, Silas and Timothy.

At the prayer meeting   Read vv.11-18.

1. What do these verses tell us about the Jewish community in Philippi (Note: ten men were needed to form a synagogue)?
2. Contrast the two women (name, occupation, status, personality).
   What do we learn about the power of God and the way He works?

In prison   Read vv.19-34.

(These verses could easily be read in dramatic form).

3. How true were the accusations made against Paul and Silas?
   Why did they not defend themselves?
4. Imagine your own reaction to unfair beating and imprisonment.
   How do you account for theirs?
5. If Paul's concern had been for himself, he would have fled as soon as the prison gates were opened. Why didn't he?
6. What caused the jailor to believe in God. Was it simply the words of Paul and Silas?
7. How was the faith of the jailor — and of Lydia — demonstrated? (vv.15,33-34)
   Try to think of modern equivalents.

Released   Read vv.35-40.

8. Why did Paul stand up for his rights? (Was he looking to the future position of Christians in Philippi?)

Conclusion

Paul and Silas had every reason to be afraid, but in fact it was the 'powerful' people who were, the jailor (v.29) and the magistrates (v.38). When Paul wrote a letter to Lydia the slave girl, the jailor and his family, and other Christians in Philippi he spoke of the secret of this carefree life. Read Philippians **4**.4-7.

How can we know this same 'peace of God' in every situation?

Outline 10:

Above the circumstances—not under them!

Philippians 1.3-26

Too often Christians allow the circumstances in which they live to dictate the way they live. The pendulum swings from being 'on top of the world' one day to being 'down in the dumps' the next. It is even possible to think that God is at the mercy of circumstances and can only be expected to be at work when they are favourable.

The readers of this letter are anxious for the author's welfare because of his situation. See verses 7, 13, 17. Paul has recently come to trial in connection with his appeal to Caesar and is at present in prison awaiting the verdict — acquittal or death. Such circumstances would surely (a) hinder the preaching of the Gospel, and (b) dishearten the servant of Christ.

But— *verses 12-14*

1. In what two ways does Paul say Christ's work is advancing under these circumstances?
2. Could the earliest days of the church at Philippi be classified as a similar example to this? See previous outline (no. 9).
3. Discuss the circumstances in which you have been placed to serve Christ. Can you see any ways in which He may be using those circumstances 'to advance the Gospel'?

verses 19-26

4. Why is Paul rejoicing rather than worrying in circumstances like these?
5. What does he want to happen, whatever the result of his trial?
6. Which would he choose to be the outcome of the trial? Which does he think will be God's will for him, and why?

7. Discuss how verse 21 should affect the way you live as a Christian in your particular situation. Is it really possible for a Christian today to rejoice in every situation?

Paul's living with Christ has freed him from having to worry about himself. So he is free to care for the Christians at Philippi.

verses 3-11

8. Why does he have a special concern for them?
9. How does he express his care of them?
10. What does he want to happen to them?

Outline 11:

Getting on with Other people

Philippians 1.27-30 and 2.1-18

Here Paul tells the Christians at Philippi what he expects of them as a group living in fellowship together. His advice, instruction and encouragement is given in the context of a hymn (2.5-11), praising the Lord Jesus Christ who embodies the characteristics and behaviour he wants to see in them. He appeals to them to aim for unity in the face of hostility from the surrounding pagan world and strife among themselves. This is advice which any group of Christians might well take to heart. Paul sets his standard in the opening sentence, 'Only let your manner of life be worthy of the gospel of Christ'.

1.27-2.4

1. The Christians at Philippi are surrounded by a hostile world. What qualities does Paul want to see in their lives?
2. What advice does Paul give the Philippians to remedy the strife among themselves?
3. Is there any way in which your group could be said to be (a) surrounded by hostility, (b) disunited? How would you apply Paul's advice to your situation?

2.5-11

4. Make a list of the things said about Christ in verses 6-11. How does Christ's example illustrate the attitude desired by Paul in verses 2-4?

2.12-18

5. Pick out from verses 14-18 the characteristics that Christians should show in their lives. How do they affect the behaviour of (a) the individual, (b) the group?
6. What do verses 12-13 say about the way in which the Christian life-style of the individual and the group is to be achieved?

Preparation (ii)

Work steadily through the outline. We have seen that the leader's task is to ask stimulating questions which make people think for themselves: he must not do all their thinking for them. But there are good and bad questions. 'What does the passage say about . . . ?' or 'What do you think verse 8 really means?' are much more likely to produce a useful answer than 'Has anyone anything to say about this passage?', to which the unspoken answer is usually 'no'. The questions in these Outlines have been framed to bring out the essential teaching of the passage and the relation of each section to the whole. Be prepared to put the questions into your own words, if they sound stilted to you, but think very carefully before you actually substitute other questions. You will, of course, have to be prepared to ask questions if the group is slow to find the full answer. Above all, remember that you cannot pass on to others what you have not fully and clearly comprehended yourself.

The planned questions in these Outlines are not isolated, and the leader must understand the progressive line of thought if he is to lead the group to the final conclusion. In this he will be assisted by the sub-headings of the Outlines, which he can announce to the group at the beginning of the study, so that they will be able to follow throughout.

Outline 12:

Religious or Christian?

Philippians 3.2-14

Paul has heard that certain Christian preachers are likely to be visiting Philippi and teaching that it is essential for a man to be circumcised according to the Jewish Law if he is going to be saved. He warns these Gentile Christians to be on their guard against false teaching of this kind, and reminds them that the essence of Christianity is not performance or religious ritual ('confidence in the flesh') but a personal relationship with the risen Jesus ('glory in Christ Jesus').

Write the following list on a blackboard or piece of card, and ask the group to discuss in pairs which, if any, of these is essential if a person is to be a true Christian — saved, acceptable to God, sure of forgiveness and Heaven:

> baptism
> charitable activities
> telling other people about Jesus
> speaking in tongues
> obeying the commandments
> believing in the Creed

After brief reporting back, work out the warning which Paul gives the Philippians in verses 2-6. In what way did Paul at one time share the attitude of these teachers, and to what extent is the above list similar to the list in verses 5-6?

Paul contrasts this 'religious' way of living with 'Christian' living summed up in verse 8 as 'knowing Christ Jesus my Lord'. Discuss what this means and why it is so different from the attitude of the false teachers. Frome verses 7-14 work out:

1. What Paul is determined to discard to enjoy this relationship.

2. What he has received through this relationship.
3. What he expects to share in as this relationship develops.
4. What he is prepared to admit about this relationship.
5. What he will need to do if this relationship is to mature.

Remember that Paul is writing the end of his life, as an experienced Christian leader; yet notice his ambition and the enthusiasm he possesses for achieving it. How can Christians guard against losing these two things as they grow older?

When the group meets (i)

(a) Begin promptly. If you always wait, people will get the 'late' habit.

(b) Open with prayer. We must seek the enlightenment of the Holy Spirit.

(c) If this is the first study of a series, give a brief introduction. Subsequent studies will probably need some sort of link with the previous one.

(d) Give the title to the whole outline and read out the section headings, so that the group can see the course the study is going to take.

(e) The passage should be read in sections and each section discussed before passing on to the next. Ask a different person to read each one.

(f) In your leadership, avoid dullness at all costs! Be inspiring, and thrilled with the passage yourself. At the same time be humble: you and the group are learning together and you must not assume an attitude of superiority. The answers you have worked out may not be the only ones — or even the right ones!

Outline 13:

Going forward

Philippians 3.14-4.9.

At the end of the previous study we looked at how Paul strove to attain spiritual maturity. If he, an experienced Christian, needed to do this, how much more his less experienced readers — then, and now! So sure is he that there is only one way forward, that he is confident that God will correct false ideas (**3**.15)

Read the whole section.

A. Power of Example (3.17; 4.9.)

Why was Paul entitled to write this? Why was it important to do so? What does it imply concerning his own life?

Leader:remember the particular calling of an apostle — see Ephesians **2**.20 — and the fact that the N.T. that we now have was not as yet written.

B. Concern for others (4.2-5)

In **4**.2, Paul makes a personal appeal to two women who have a disagreement. What else do these verses imply about them? If a similar disagreement were to continue unchecked between two of your own members, what would be the likely effects (a) on them (b) on the group (c) on outsiders?

If reconciliation is to be achieved, what two things (at least) seem to be necessary?

C. 'We' and 'they' (3.18-20).

In a word, what would you say is the main factor that distinguishes the 'they' from the 'we'? In the light of verse 19, think of examples in the realms of school, college, and work, of those 'whose lives make them enemies of Christ's death on the cross' (TEV).

Leader: note (a) the strength of Paul's feeling here and (b) the strength of God's transforming power.

D. Personal development (4.4-8)

(a) in heart: In the first century there was plenty of reason for Christians to be disheartened and fearful. How can these fears be counteracted, and with what results?

(b) in mind: 'THINK' . . . Make a list of the group's suggestions of at least one thing for each description given in verse 8. Read them out at 15 — second intervals, so that everyone can *think* positively about them.

In Conclusion.

The leader could offer a prayer including these two commands: . . . 'hold true to what we have already attained . . .' (**3**.16) . . . 'stand firm in the Lord' . . . (**4**.1.)

Outline 14:

Why worry?

Philippians **4**.6-20.

Introduction

Paul's circumstances in prison, gave him every justification to feel depressed and discontented. Personal contentment however, was not Paul's aim, but was a by-product of his obedience to God's will.

Read the section together.

A. Divide into groups of three or four. Ask each group to write down what Paul says are the right attitudes to

  (a) Prayer
  (b) Thinking
  (c) Possessions and circumstances

and how these attitudes can be achieved (e.g. vv. 7, 9, 13, 19).
To save time, each group could deal with only one topic.
Report back, and discuss how our attitude to these three things will affect our contentment.

B. Select from the following questions, and discuss as many as time allows:

  (1) Would you describe contentment as an attitude or a feeling?
  (2) What reasons are there why some Christians are discontented?
  (3) What would you say to a Christian who was always grumbling?
  (4) Are some people by nature more contented than others?

(Note: The substance of this outline also appears in the series 'Following Christ' as outline no. 19.; it is included here to give adequate coverage to Paul's letter to the Philippians.)

When the group meets (ii)

(g) *Stick to the passage and beware of twisting it to suit a particular meaning. Introduce cross-references to other Scriptures only if you must.*

(h) *Make the group do the work, and do your best to draw everyone in. Appreciate every effort made, and never be 'crushing'.*

(i) *Press questions till the answer is complete: for example; 'Is there any further answer?' or 'Does it say anything more about that?' From the answers you get you will be able to judge how much of your question has been understood. You can then build on these answers to draw out more.*

(j) *Summarise each section as you go along, normally according to the headings of the outline or the introduction which you have given.*

(k) *Use the title of the study as your final summary: it will usually be in the form of a question. Get the group to say what answer the passage has given to it.*

(l) *Wherever possible, end with a few minutes of open prayer, during which members of the group, having their Bibles open before them, can be encouraged to 'pray in' the lessons that have been learnt.*

Outline 15:

Who is Jesus?

Colossians 1.15-23

In writing his letter to the Colossians, Paul was anxious to correct false teachings on the subject of who Jesus really was. Some people argued that He was in fact only a good man — the highest created being — but not God. In this section, Paul sets out clearly the true nature of Jesus and the work He came to do.

Read the section.

As when Paul was writing his letter, so today many people say that Jesus was merely a good man. (e.g. Jehovah's Witnesses, etc.)

1. What does Paul say in these verses about the real nature of Jesus (vv.15-20). (Note to the leader: 'first-born of all creation' (v.15) does not mean that Jesus was Himself 'created' but rather that He existed before creation began. See N.E.B. or J. B. Phillips' translations. Look at John 1.1-3.)
2. In your own words, explain simply Paul's answer to the question 'Who is Jesus?'
3. In what way is Christ's work in the Universe continuing today? (v.17).
4. What does the picture of the head and the body teach us about the right relationship between Jesus and His people? (v.18).
5. Verse 18 says that Jesus is 'first in everything'.
   If this statement is true in the lives of individual Christians, what difference will it make in our attitude towards:-
   (a) our job?
   (b) our leisure?
   (c) our friendships?

In verses 19-20, Paul explains that in Christ, it is possible for man to be at peace with God again. (i.e. reconciled).

6. How was this reconciliation between God and man made possible? (see verses 20, 22 and also verses 13, 14.)
   Paul explains that there are definite consequences for the believer as a result of Christ's death.
7. In your own words, explain what these consequences are (vv.21-23).
8. Are there any conditions attached to God's offer of reconciliation that we need to fulfil if we are to accept it? (v.23).

Outline 16:

Grow This Way

Colossians 1.28-2.15

Read the section.
Questions for discussion:

1. What was Paul's aim in preaching and teaching? (1.28) (Note that the aim was for every Christian to be mature.) How does Paul see this maturity being made evident in Christian's lives (2.2).

2. What are the origins of all truth?
   Why must we ensure that our faith is founded on correct facts? (2.4 and 8) (Leader: include being able to recognize 'smooth talkers' and non-christian ways of thinking).
   Can you think of any modern examples, and why they might be dangerous to the Christians? (e.g. 'Do your own thing').

3. How does Paul describe a mature Christian? (5-7) What help does he give to the Colossians about reaching maturity? (5-7)

4. Why must Christ be at the centre of the Christian view of life? (8-10) Ye are 'complete in Him'. (v.10) In what ways are we 'complete in Christ' — spiritually? morally? and mentally?
   List the implications of our 'union with Christ' (vv.11-15). (Circumcision was the Jew's outward sign that they were God's own people.)

5. Supplementary question. What should a mature Christian think and do if he

   (a) fails an examination?
   (b) is offered some responsibility?
   (c) overhears a friend being sarcastic about him?

Outline 17:

Living This Way

Colossians 3.1-17

Read the section.
Questions for discussion:

1. What facts can and should influence us as Christians in our attitude to life? (vv.1-4).
   What things are damaging to a Christian's life and why? (vv.5-11).
   What place does national pride and educational status have in the Christian life? (v.11)
2. Having emphasized the things that need removing from a Christian's life, Paul goes on positively to list the qualities that a Christian should aim for. As you make a list, say what difference each quality should make to (a) the individual (b) the church.
   What part must we play in acquiring these qualities, and what part does God play? (vv.15-16)
3. What practical implications does it have, if we try to do 'all things in the Name of the Lord Jesus'? (v.17)
   Would this cause us to question certain activities? Give examples.
4. Supplementary question:
   It is easy to agree with Paul when he says that love is the greatest Christian virtue (v.14). But supposing you knew that breakfast was at 8.15, and you came down virtuously at 8.35, having been tidying your room, to meet an unwarranted (as you thought) rebuke. You felt annoyed and vented your irritation on your sister. She retaliated, and you left the house feeling that everyone was against you.... This process could have been arrested if you had acted in love. Exactly how, at each stage?

Outline 18:

Slavery Transformed

Philemon

Paul wrote this private letter from prison in Rome to his wealthy friend, Philemon, who was a member of the church at Colossae. In it, he asked him to forgive his runaway slave, Onesimus, whose name meant 'useful'. Onesimus had stolen from his master but, after disappearing, had come under Paul's influence and had become a Christian.

Paul sent Onesimus back to Philemon with this plea for mercy. For even though Philemon was a Christian and a member of the Colossian church, the Roman law allowed a master to take almost unlimited vengeance on a runaway slave. Paul had clearly become very fond of Onesimus.

Should Paul have used this opportunity to condemn slavery? Does he appear simply to go along with the social pattern of his day? These questions may be uppermost in our minds, yet it is important to recognize that:

(a) The old Testament system of slavery was very different from that practised by the Romans, in that it was based on God's concern for the slave seen as a person, not as property, and (b) Paul shows that the legal relationship between a slave and his master can be transformed by the fact that they are *brothers* in Christ.

Questions for discussion:

1. What two features did Paul especially commend in Philemon? (v.5) In what ways was Paul asking Philemon to demonstrate these two Christian virtues?

2. How had Onesimus changed in becoming a Christian? Should people always show a radical change of character when they begin to trust Christ?
3. How was Paul able to serve God from prison? Can you think of any modern counterparts (those imprisoned for their faith) and how they have served God? What do we learn from their examples?
4. What has Paul to say about the relationship of master and slave? What application has this in human relationships today?

Project

Prepare a dramatised version of the Onesimus story.
Introduce various characters; fellow slave, Paul, Philemon.

The shy, the over-talkative . . .

(a) Encourage the new or shy member by asking him perhaps to read a particular verse (half the battle is won the first time he opens his mouth!)
(b) Restrain the too-talkative member by saying, 'Could someone who has not yet spoken tell us . . .?' If this person persists, speak to him privately.
(c) Bring back to the passage those who wander away from it. If somebody makes an irrelevant contribution, ask him gently which verse in the passage he had in mind.

Outline 19:

Full of Confidence

2 Timothy 1.

It is very difficult to give your life to anyone or anything unless you have an increasing confidence in the truth or trustworthiness of the person or the cause. Any kind of commitment is costly — sooner or later — but we're prepared to pay the cost if it's worth it! Paul talks in this chapter to Timothy, encouraging him to grow in confidence and gives himself as an example.

1. Of what importance to him is Timothy's background? How does your background help you as a Christian?
2. Paul seems to lay a lot of weight on Timothy's dedication to the task of leading the Church. (1 Tim. 4:14, 2 Tim. 1:6) How would the three evidences of the Spirit in his life give him confidence for his responsibilities as leader? What situations in your school or church will you need these for?
3. Getting our situation into perspective often helps us to 'see beyond the trees to the wood'. What factors does Paul mention in vv.6-12 that should encourage Timothy to see the Gospel and his calling in a broad perspective?
4. Paul mentions several times that he and others have had to suffer for the Gospel. Vv.9-11 describe the Good News. What is so offensive about it? Do your friends struggle with it?
5. Vv.11-14. Where did Paul's confidence lie? What other suggestions did Paul give Timothy that would encourage his confidence?
6. How do the last few verses of this chapter fit in? How can we encourage those who lead us?

Some other problems

(d) If time is running out, 'telescope' parts of the outline, but still make sure that you cover the ground. Foreseeing the possibility of this, plan beforehand which parts of the outline you will summarise briefly if necessary, so that you can come on to later questions which will be put to the group.

(e) Sometimes there may be disagreement amongst members of the group. If so, summarise the points of view and pass on.

(f) Some groups are slower than others to get moving on Bible study. This problem can often be overcome by asking a pair of members to prepare — one to lead, and the other to back up.

Outline 20:

On Active Service

2 Timothy 2.

Christians who wish to be leaders 'desire a good thing' !
But the character and quality of life required need to be
reckoned with. Paul is asking for a total commitment, not
affected by social or intellectual pressures, but by the
person of Christ, his words, standards and love.

1. Vv.20,21. To what extent are we responsible for how
   much God uses us?
2. What directions do vv.1-6 give to someone preparing
   for a position of spiritual responsibility? What qualities of life are implied in the three examples of
   discipline? How would you recognize a faithful man?
3. V.9. Paul still considered himself to be in active service. What three facts kept him going? Where does
   the memory help here?
4. As a leader, what one says is very important. Vv.14-19
   and 23-26 use several speaking verbs. Make a chart
   of these
      speaker   verb   to whom   message   result
   Where do discussions fit here? What must the leader
   be able to do?
5. What you are shows in what you say. How can you
   prepare yourself now for active Christian living and
   service? Give up-to-date examples of v.22.

Focus on what can be understood
*From time to time, difficulties are bound to arise which
cannot for the moment be solved within the group.
Concentrate rather on what can be understood than on
the problems themselves, so that the thread of the study
is not lost. Any matters of particular interest can be
agreeably set on one side with a view to devoting a further study to them, or possibly giving them to a visiting
speaker who asks for a subject.*

Outline 21:

Fully Qualified

2 Timothy 3.

Paul is anxious, in this chapter, to give Timothy some idea of what he is likely to face as the pastor of the church. He describes not only what the world is like, but also what the false Christians are likely to do. He urges Timothy to observe his example of leadership, to be consistent, and to use what has been provided for him to make himself a fully qualified leader.

1. *Times of stress.* Which of the things mentioned in vv.1-5 would you pick out as the basic sin, which is the root of all others? What is sin? In what forms do we find the things mentioned in the list here in the world today?
2. *Avoid these people.* What characteristics are referred to in vv.6-9 that would not permit pseudo-Christians to become qualified leaders? How would vv.16,17 help to detect where they have gone wrong?
3. *Observe Paul.* Paul was chosen by God as an apostle. He gives us in vv.10,11, a picture of how he coped with life. In pairs, study the verses and prepare an account of his experiences as if you were Paul. Paul was not always like that. Discuss how vv.16,17 might have helped to change him in his early Christian life, so that he could react as a Christian later on.
4. *Qualifying.*
   (a) Background. What do vv. 14, 15 say about how we should make use of our early training as a Christian? To what extent are we responsible for our salvation?
   (b) Why is consistent reading of the Bible important to a Christian? Where can you get teaching from?

(c) 'I am what I am. I can't change.' Break up into groups and think of examples to disprove that statement in the light of vv. 16, 17.

5. What qualities of a leader are mentioned in this chapter, and how can these become a part of your life?

Outline 22:

The Last Word

2 Timothy 4.

It is rare for most of us to look back over our lives and take stock. Paul here gives us insight into his thinking just before he died. His final instructions to Timothy are based on profound doctrinal statements; his attitudes to his co-workers on their co-operation with him and their continuing in the faith; and his attitudes to his own life and his desire to do everything well and faithfully.

Paul's charge to Timothy.

1. How urgent were his instructions?
2. What were the three motivations for service? How should these motivate us?
3. List the words that Paul uses for conveying the Gospel or its impact on the hearers. How do they differ in meaning?
4. In pairs, explain to each other to what extent each of you consider these to be your responsibility.

Finished.

5. How real to Paul is heaven, the return of Christ and the Kingdom? To what extent do we live in the light of these facts?
6. What is Paul's attitude to death?
7. What is implied in his summary of his life? Is he being realistic?

The Roll of Honour.

8. What qualities did Paul note in the men he mentioned.

9. Why would he not have been free to write the injunction that he gave to Timothy to each of these?

Group preparation

A study will always be more profitable if the members of the group have done some preparation beforehand. Encourage them at least to read the passage. If a group is slow to talk it may help if beforehand you allot each question to a different member, who must come prepared to give an answer to it. These answers can then be used as a basis for discussion as you go along.